Wizard Crafts

23 spellbinding toys, gifts, costumes and party decorations

Heidi Boyd

NORTH LIGHT BOOKS
CINCINNATI, OHIO
www.artistsnetwork.com

Wizard Crafts: 23 spellbinding toys, gifts, costumes and party decorations. Copyright © 2004 by Heidi Boyd. Printed in Singapore. All rights reserved. The patterns and drawings in the book are for the personal use of the reader. By permission of the author and publisher, they may be either hand-traced or photocopied to make single copies, but under no circumstances may they be resold or republished. It is permissible for the purchaser to make the projects contained herein and sell them at fairs, bazaars and craft shows. No other part of this book may be reproduced in any form or by any electronic or mechanical means, including information storage and retrieval systems, without permission in writing from the publisher, except by a reviewer, who may quote a brief passage in a review. Published by North Light Books, an imprint of F+W Publications, Inc., 4700 East Galbraith Road, Cincinnati, Ohio 45236. (800) 289-0963. First edition.

08 07 06 05 04   5 4 3 2 1

Library of Congress Cataloging-in-Publication Data

Boyd, Heidi.
   Wizard crafts: 23 spellbinding toys, gifts, costumes and party decorations / by Heidi Boyd.--1st ed.
      p.cm.
   Includes index.
   ISBN 1-58180-437-7 (pbk. : alk. paper)
   1. Handicraft--Juvenile literature. 2. Wizards--Juvenile literature.
   I. Title.

TT190.B68 2004
745.5--dc22
                                    2003064902

Editor: Jolie Lamping Roth
Designer: Stephanie Strang
Illustrator for pages 12, 38, 58, 72: Heidi Boyd
Layout Artist: Kathy Gardner
Production Coordinator: Sara Dumford
Photographers: Christine Polomsky and Tim Grondin
Photo Stylist: Jan Nickum

metric conversion chart

TO CONVERT	TO	MULTIPLY BY
Inches	Centimeters	2.54
Centimeters	Inches	0.4
Feet	Centimeters	30.5
Centimeters	Feet	0.03
Yards	Meters	0.9
Meters	Yards	1.1
Sq. Inches	Sq. Centimeters	6.45
Sq. Centimeters	Sq. Inches	0.16
Sq. Feet	Sq. Meters	0.09
Sq. Meters	Sq. Feet	10.8
Sq. Yards	Sq. Meters	0.8
Sq. Meters	Sq. Yards	1.2
Pounds	Kilograms	0.45
Kilograms	Pounds	2.2
Ounces	Grams	28.4
Grams	Ounces	0.04

ABOUT THE AUTHOR

Artist Heidi Boyd creates innovative craft projects for children, emphasizing the elements of surprise and accessibility. In addition to *Wizard Crafts*, Heidi has authored *Fairy Crafts* and *Pet Crafts*, also published by North Light Books. She's contributed proprietary projects to the kid's sections of *Better Homes and Gardens*, *Crayola Kids* and *FamilyFun* magazines. With a degree in fine arts, Heidi has been an art instructor to children in schools and art centers for over a decade, while pursuing her vocation as an illustration artist. She lives in Maine with her husband and two sons.

DEDICATED
TO THE THREE WIZARDS IN MY LIFE:
Jon, Jasper and Elliot, who kindle magic in my heart every day.

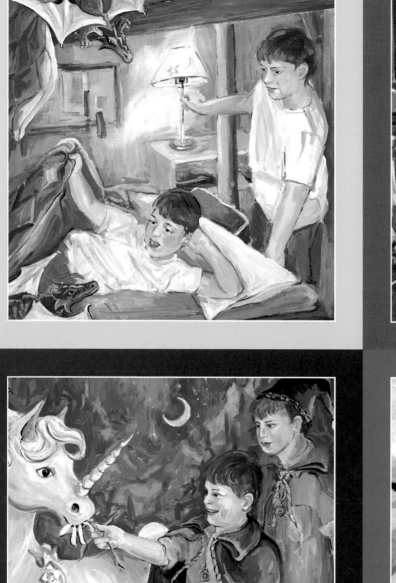

table of CONTENTS

INTRODUCTION

Alakazoom! Alakazam! Join the adventure and ride on a dragon's back through a magical world in search of a crystal ball. Creatures and magical objects that before existed only in the realm of your child's imagination become tangible in the craft projects that follow each stage of the adventure.

Making wizard and dragon crafts with your child will provide hours of fun and valuable learning experiences along the way. Science and art come together when your child discovers that oil and water don't mix in the potion bottle, learns how a prism refracts light in the kaleidoscope, and explores the magnetic force that invisibly pulls the puppets across the stage.

Bring magic into birthday celebrations and drama to dress up play. Host a wizardly celebration where guests craft a game that yields sweet rewards. The showstopping costumes are deceivingly simple, assembled over clothing to ensure both success and a comfortable fit. Transform everyday materials like a chopstick into a magic wand, or a soda bottle into a lantern, to make perfect accessories for any disguise.

Share your child's love of dragons and unicorns by making custom gifts together for friends and family—inexpensive and beautiful solutions for last-minute gifts or inspiration to make treasured keepsakes. Every step is clearly photographed and paired with detailed instructions, so making these projects with your child is almost as easy as saying "Abracadabra!" Cast a spell of amazement on your children and bring to their fingertips the world of magical crafts that will be the inspiration for hours of creative play.

★ Heidi

getting started

★

The materials lists in this book feature standard arts and crafts supplies that should be readily available. Some equipment requires adult supervision, so please take a moment to read the following before you start crafting with your child.

Basic Tools

A **hot glue gun** is used in some of the projects. Please supervise your children when using a glue gun. I suggest a low-temperature smaller-size glue gun, which will be easier for older children to handle. The low setting will help prevent burns. Take the time to instruct them on the hazards of using this tool. If you have reservations about using hot glue, I would suggest using Beacon's Kids Choice Glue as an alternative. It's thick, bonds quickly (although still not as quickly as hot glue) and often has a stronger adhesion after it's dried.

hot glue gun

Using a **sewing machine** is an exciting skill for an older child to acquire with adult supervision. The wizard cape (page 42) has two straight seams and is a great beginning machine-stitching project. Please be sure to sit with your child at the machine and discuss safety precautions, especially keeping fingers clear of the needle. The belly of the Dragon Costume (page 48) is more difficult because of the folded layers of fabric and sweatshirt. Your child will learn a great deal from being your assistant in cutting, pinning, hand stitching and stuffing the Dragon Costume.

For the projects using polymer clay (the Spell Book and Bookmark [pages 76-77] and the Dragon Crystal Ball Holder [page 80]) an **oven** is needed to cure the clay. Let the pieces cool completely before handling them.

The Magical T-Shirts (page 84) will require the use of an **iron**. Please exercise caution when using the iron.

If your child would like to help with the projects involving the oven or iron, consider having your child prepare the pieces for you to bake or iron as needed.

Also, materials such as paint markers and adhesives (like the ones used in the Cauldron [page 19], Red Sparkle Potion [page 20], the Wand [page 42], and the Jeweled Goblets [page 66]) should be used in a well-ventilated area. Please supervise your children when using these materials.

☆ ☆ ☆ **PLEASE NOTE: The projects in this book are intended for older children. Many contain small parts that are not suitable for children under three years of age.**

sewing machine

iron

11

THE MAGICAL WORLD APPEARS

The boys were out in the woods behind their house mixing concoctions of seedpods, feathers and trailing vines in a black pot. They were startled when all of a sudden smoke arose from the pot. "Wow, it looks like a unicorn!" Jasper exclaimed. "What did you put in there?" The image dissipated, and the brothers unsuccessfully tried to re-create the potion. Tired, they retreated to the shade of the tree house.

Elliot held the kaleidoscope they kept by the window up to the light. The colors swirled a brilliant blue and then suddenly switched to a scarlet red. "Wow, Jasper, you have to see this."

"Elliot, I've looked through that kaleidoscope a hundred times. I'm still trying to figure out what you put in the pot." Elliot came across the room and insisted. "Jasper, I'm serious. You won't believe this." Jasper reluctantly held the scope to his eyes and was shocked when the swirls of colors appeared.

Later that evening in their bunk beds the boys were still trying to understand the visions, wondering if they were just illusions. Elliot felt something nudge his foot and demanded, "Jasper, stop it."

Just then Jasper felt a tap on his shoulder. "Elliot, I didn't do anything. Cut it out."

Elliot ordered, "Jasper, turn on the light, right now!" Jasper turned on the lamp. The boys gasped, "Topaz?" "Garnet?" as they watched their stuffed dragons duck under the covers, shielding their blue and red eyes from the light.

Timidly the dragons emerged, blinking their gleaming eyes against the light. "You have to help us." The boys stared frozen in shock. "This way," they motioned, "we'll show you."

enchanting TOYS

WHO DOESN'T LOVE FUN AND GAMES? IN THIS CHAP-
TER YOU'LL FIND A CAULDRON WHERE YOU AND
YOUR FRIENDS CAN MIX UP CONCOCTIONS
OF PLASTIC SPIDERS AND EYEBALLS, OR A
BOTTLE OF GLITTERING POTION. AMAZE
YOUR FRIENDS WITH A LIFE-SIZE CLOMPING
DRAGON MARIONETTE OR WITH MAGNETIC
PUPPETS THAT MYSTERIOUSLY GLIDE ACROSS
THE STAGE. IF YOU SHY AWAY FROM THE SPOTLIGHT,
ENJOY A QUIET MOMENT GAZING THROUGH A KALEI-
DOSCOPE OR SNUGGLING WITH A STUFFED DRAGON.

Kaleidoscope

Hold this beautiful kaleidoscope up to the light and rotate it to watch the glass pieces shift to create beautiful swirls of color. A clear plastic candy container lets the light pass through the colored glass, and a prism of foil refracts the colored light down the length of the scope. Flip the end of the candy container open to change the combination of glass and beads. This ever-changing toy is the perfect mix of art and science.

WHAT YOU WILL NEED

- ☆ lightweight aluminum (I used ArtEmboss) or heavyweight household foil
- ☆ cardboard tube (the one included with the ArtEmboss foil is perfect)
- ☆ cardstock
- ☆ scrapbook paper
- ☆ adhesive-backed sparkle paper (I used Making Memories sparkle paper)

- ☆ glass gems, mosaic pieces and/or beads
- ☆ plastic container (I used a Tic Tac container)
- ☆ gold cord, at least 56" (1.5m)
- ☆ double-stick tape
- ☆ clear packing tape
- ☆ pencil

- ☆ tacky glue
- ☆ scissors
- ☆ ruler (1" [3cm] wide)
- ☆ drinking glass

NOTE: The foil measurement works for the tube included with the ArtEmboss foil. Any tube can be used, but a heavyweight tube makes a more durable kaleidoscope. Adjust the foil width to be three times the diameter of the selected tube plus a ½" (1cm) overlay for taping. The length of the foil should match the length of the tube.

1 Cut 3½" (9cm) of foil (shiny side up) and roll 3" (8cm) onto a 1" (3cm) wide ruler and then fold down the ½" (1cm) overlay. Unfold the foil to remove the ruler; it will have made three fold lines.

2 Use the fold lines to make the prism. Use double-stick tape to attach the ½" (1cm) overlap to the prism. Insert the foil prism into the tube.

3 Trace the bottom of a drinking glass onto cardstock. Center one end of the cardboard tube inside the circle and then trace around the tube to make a second circle inside the first. Cut out the larger circle.

4 Use a pencil tip to poke out a hole in the center of the smaller circle. Make wedges around the circle, cutting slits from the outer circle to the inner circle. Apply glue to the wedges and then position the center circle over the end of the tube. Press the glue-covered wedges down around the sides of the tube and hold them in place while the glue sets.

5 Cut a piece of scrapbook paper the length of the tube. Apply glue to the back of the paper and then roll the paper around the tube.

6 Wrap a ½" (1cm) wide piece of sparkle paper around the top of the tube. Wrap a 3" (8cm) wide piece of sparkle paper around the bottom of the tube. Slide glass gems into a small plastic container, leaving room for the pieces to shift. Wrap a strip of clear packing tape from one side of the tube across the container and back down to the other side of the tube. Cover the white plastic cap with a small strip of sparkle paper.

7 Fold a 56" (1.5m) piece of gold cord in half. Wrap it twice around the tube toward the top end and then knot.

Experiment with different translucent materials, plastic gems, cellophane and/or beads to create exciting light effects.

18

Cauldron

Transform an inexpensive Halloween castoff into a wizarding toy that will inspire imagination all year round. Just add plastic frogs, lizards, bugs and eyeballs as props, and who could resist mixing up imaginary potions in this playful cauldron.

WHAT YOU WILL NEED

☆ black plastic cauldron and stirring spoon
☆ alphabet stickers
☆ white label
☆ star-shaped rhinestones
☆ silver metallic marker
☆ tacky glue
☆ all-purpose industrial-strength craft adhesive (I used Aleene's Platinum Bond 7800 Adhesive)
☆ masking tape
☆ scissors

STEP ONE

1 Position alphabet stickers on a white label. Cut around the stickers in an irregular, cracked pattern to simulate an old weathered label. Outline the cut edge with a metallic silver marker and place the sticker on one side of the cauldron. Apply tacky glue to the edges of the label to secure.

STEP TWO

2 Use a very small bead of industrial-strength adhesive to attach the decorative rhinestones to the label and cauldron. Use short strips of masking tape to hold the rhinestones in place while the glue dries.

19

Red Sparkle Potion

This magical potion bottle demonstrates the simple chemistry phenomenon that oil and water don't mix. Every time the bottle is shaken, the oil bubbles up and sets the glittering confetti into motion. Hold the bottle to the light or place it in a windowsill to best illuminate the special effects.

WHAT YOU WILL NEED

- ☆ glass or plastic bottle with cork or tight-fitting lid
- ☆ mineral oil
- ☆ red food coloring
- ☆ white and red confetti
- ☆ all-purpose industrial-strength craft adhesive (I used Aleene's Platinum Bond 7800 Adhesive)
- ☆ water
- ☆ paper towel

T I P *The popularity of homemade bath salts and herbed olive oils has stocked both craft and import store shelves with beautiful ornamental containers. These make great potion bottles.*

1 Set the cork aside and pour mineral oil into the bottle until you reach the halfway mark. Squeeze about ten drops of red food coloring into the bottle.

2 Tip several tablespoons of red and white confetti into the bottle. Carefully fill the remaining space with water, stopping about ¼" (6mm) from the top.

3 With a paper towel, wipe the inside edge of the bottle dry. Apply glue around the sides of the cork and then firmly insert it into the top of the bottle. Apply another ring of glue around where the cork meets the glass to improve the seal. Let dry for 24 hours before shaking the bottle. Experiment with different food color and glitter combinations to create additional potion bottles.

Store your plastic spell-making ingredients in glass or plastic bottles with decorated labels made like the cauldron's. To label smaller bottles, spell ingredients in alphabet stickers on a metal-rimmed tag. Wrap a ¼" (6mm) ribbon around the bottle's neck, and then thread the ribbon ends through the punched hole in the tag and knot the ends together.

flies

SNAKE EYES

worm

newt

Stuffed Dragon

A new twist on the sock monkey, this charming stuffed dragon is assembled almost entirely from socks. Any child would enjoy playing with this pet, but making it is just as much fun. It's a perfect beginning hand-sewing project for an older child. With your help, a younger child can choose colors, stuff fiberfill, cut out felt pieces and position the eyes, ears, feet, fringe, nostrils and tail.

WHAT YOU WILL NEED

☆ three bobby socks
☆ four infant socks
☆ fiberfill
☆ scraps of stiffened felt
☆ 1 yard (1m) of 45" (114cm) wide tulle

☆ plastic eyes made especially for stuffed toys (packaged with backings to hold them in place)
☆ two glitter pom-poms
☆ 18" (46cm) gold fringe

☆ scissors
☆ hot glue gun
☆ needle and thread
☆ patterns (page 86)

1 Stuff the three bobby socks and four infant socks with fiberfill. The bobby socks will be the dragon's head, body and tail. The infant socks will be the legs.

2 Use the eye pattern to cut two felt eyes out of stiffened felt. Carefully make a snip in the center of each felt eye with the tip of your scissors. Push a plastic eye through the slit in each felt eye. Select one stuffed bobby sock to be the head. Hold the back of the plastic eye in the hand that is going to work inside the sock. Push the plastic end of the eye through the outside of the sock and then hold it in place by sliding the back piece up the plastic end inside the sock. Repeat the process on the other side of the sock to position the second eye. Note: If a run forms in the sock when you insert the eye, stop the damage with a drop of hot glue.

3 Connect the body by pulling the cuff of the tail sock over the toe of the body sock, then hand stitch around the cuff to hold it in place. Pull the cuff of the body sock over the neck of the head and then stitch it in place. The stuffing should be completely concealed inside the connected socks.

4 Turn the dragon body over to attach the legs. Hand sew the tops of all four infant socks to the dragon's belly.

5 Fold the tulle, then position the wing pattern against the fold and cut out. Repeat three more times to make a total of four wings. Unfold each wing and stack the layers of tulle together. Starting at the top, accordion fanfold the length of the wings. Hand stitch down through the center of the folded wings to secure them to the top of the dragon's back.

6 Use the patterns to cut the ears, mouth, teeth and tail tip out of stiffened felt scraps. Hot glue the tail tip over the end of the sock tail, the ears to either side of the head, and then glue the teeth followed by the mouth to the end of the head.

7 Use the claw pattern to cut sixteen claws out of felt scraps. Hot glue four claws onto each foot. Position three of the claws to face front and the fourth claw to face back.

8 Hot glue two pom-pom nostrils above the mouth. Hot glue the end of the fringe to the base of the felt tail tip. Continue gluing the fringe up the dragon's back, twisting it between each spot of glue.

24

Magnetic Puppet Stage

Move puppets as if by magic! Hold a magnetic wand inside the opening at the back of the box and watch your puppets (see pages 26–33) glide across the stage.

(see pages 26–33)

WHAT YOU WILL NEED

- ☆ shoe box, 11¾" x 8½" x 4½" (30cm x 22cm x 11cm)
- ☆ half sheet of black posterboard
- ☆ 12" (30cm) of 2" (5cm) wide red fringe
- ☆ 25" (64cm) of 2" (5cm) wide black fringe
- ☆ double-stick tape
- ☆ craft glue
- ☆ scissors
- ☆ magnetic wands
- ☆ pattern (page 87)

NOTE: Measurements may vary depending on the size of the shoe box you use.

STEP ONE

1 Cut one long side off the back of the shoe box and the matching edge off the lid. Replace the lid and then invert the box and lid so the bottom of the box becomes the stage floor. Using the pattern, cut the stage front out of black posterboard. Use double-stick tape to attach red fringe along the top of the opening. Fold the posterboard back on either side of the stage. Place the bottom edge of the stage sides in between the lid and the box.

2 Wrap a long strip of double-stick tape around the three sides of the lid. Press the black fringe into the tape. Apply craft glue to the cut ends of the fringe to help prevent them from unraveling.

STEP TWO

Magnetic Wizard
Puppet

The wizard puppet is sure to cast
a magical spell over your audience.
With flowing robes, pointed hat and star
wand, he's ready to tame a fierce dragon.

WHAT YOU WILL NEED

☆ 3¾" (10cm) doll pin (standard size)

☆ 3 oz. (85g) purple air-dry modeling material (I used Crayola Model Magic), plus some scraps of yellow and white

☆ 7" (18cm) piece of thin chenille stem (match color to skin tone)

☆ 1¾" (4cm) piece of thin chenille stem, purple

☆ acrylic paint (in skin tone)

☆ two 4mm wiggly eyes

☆ ¾" (2cm) round magnet

☆ black colored pencil

☆ tacky glue

☆ double-stick mounting tape

☆ small paintbrush

TIP

Model Magic is a modeling material that's fun and easy for kids to manipulate, but because it's fast drying, work quickly and keep unused portions tightly wrapped.

26

1 Paint the round head of the doll pin with skin tone acrylic paint. After the paint has dried, use a colored pencil to draw a nose and mouth on the bottom half of the head. Use craft glue to glue the eyes above the nose.

2 Cut a 7" (18cm) section of matching skin tone chenille stem for the arms. Wrap the center of the chenille stem around the front of the pin. Bring the ends together behind the doll pin and twist them at the back. Bring the arms back to the front and bend them at the elbows.

3 Use most of a 3 oz. (85g) pack of purple air-dry modeling material to wrap around the doll pin and arms, leaving enough purple left over to make the hat in step 6. Conceal all but the chenille hands, doll pin head and base. Mold the purple clay into a robe by massing the clay at the sleeve and hem ends.

4 Roll a coil of yellow modeling material and wrap it around the waist for a sash. Form two egg-shaped balls of yellow clay and then press them flat. Slide a disk onto each hand and then press the yellow clay against the purple cuffs.

5 Wrap white modeling material around the wooden head for hair. Mold a long triangular beard and wrap it under the wizard's mouth. Press the length of the beard against the robe.

6 Use the leftover scraps of purple modeling material from the robe to mold a pointed hat. Roll a coil of yellow and wrap it around the hat.

7 Use a small piece of mounting tape to attach a round magnet on the bottom of the finished puppet. Make sure all the magnets used for the puppets have the same polarization so they can be activated by the magnetic wands (see the materials list for the Magnetic Puppet Stage on page 25).

8 Roll a scrap of white modeling material into a ball the size of a cranberry. Pinch five points out of the ball to make a star shape. Insert a 1¾" (4cm) piece of chenille stem into the bottom. Fold over the ends of each arm to make a ⅛" (3mm) hook. Slide the wand end into either of the newly formed hands.

The king rules the stage with a scepter and the queen rules with a flower. Don't be fooled by appearances; the puppets' hands are easily adjustable so props can be changed in an instant. If the queen gets a hold of the wizard's wand, she might rule with a magic spell!

The king and queen are constructed like the wizard, except for the following variations: Leave their heads unpainted. Use red colored pencil to make the queen's mouth and blush her cheeks. Wrap tan chenille stem arms around the pin before dressing the queen in an orange clay dress and the king in blue robes.

Frame the king's head with black clay hair and a beard. Use yellow clay to trim the queen's dress and give her a generous head of hair. Crown the king with a large yellow clay crown and the queen with a white tiara (she has matching pearls around her neck, too). Use leftover scraps to top a tan chenille scepter for the king and orange chenille flower for the queen.

Magnetic Dragon
Puppet

This dragon will add drama to your production.
His imposing red and yellow body, large
eyes and white teeth will command
your audience's attention.

WHAT YOU WILL NEED

- ☆ 3³/₄" (10cm) doll pin (standard size)
- ☆ 3 oz. (85g) red, 1¹/₂ oz. (43g) yellow and scraps of white air-dry modeling material (I used Crayola Model Magic)
- ☆ one 5¹/₂" (14cm) piece and one 6¹/₄" (16cm) piece of red chenille stem
- ☆ two oval wiggly eyes (smallest size available)

- ☆ ³/₄" (2cm) round magnet
- ☆ double-stick mounting tape
- ☆ plastic modeling knife (or butter knife)
- ☆ toothpick

1 Wrap the center of the 5½" (14cm) chenille stem around the top of the doll pin just under the head. Bring the ends together at the front of the pin and then twist them together. Fold each end back toward the doll pin to make a thicker arm. Wrap the center of the 6¼" (16cm) stem around the bottom of the doll pin. Bring the ends together and twist like the arms, only this time accordion fold each end into three toes to make the feet.

2 Cover the length of the doll pin with red modeling material, avoiding the chenille stem arms and feet. Pinch extra clay to the bottom to form the dragon's tail. Shape an elongated head and then slice the jaw into two separate pieces with a plastic knife. Push the shaped head over the top of the doll pin.

3 Press an eye into either side of the head. Push the modeling material around the edge of each eye to anchor it in place.

31

4 Use yellow modeling material to decorate the dragon. Mold a flat strip of yellow modeling material and press it down the dragon's belly. Press the plastic knife blade into the belly to create horizontal lines. Roll two tiny yellow balls and press them onto either side of the nose for nostrils. Roll the remaining modeling material into a long thin coil. Starting at the end of the nose, press one end of the coil down the center of the head. Continue pressing the coil down the length of the back and tail, pinching the coil into small spikes as you work.

5 Roll scraps of white modeling material into two thin coils. Position the first coil around the top of the mouth and the second around the bottom. Press the end of a toothpick into the white modeling material to make teeth indentations.

6 Use a small strip of mounting tape to attach a round magnet to the bottom of the dragon. Make sure all the magnets used for the puppets have the same polarization so they can be activated by the magnetic wands (see the materials list for the Magnetic Puppet Stage on page 25).

TIP

A castle stage is easy to make. Simply substitute gray posterboard for black and then use markers to outline large stone bricks onto the gray background. If your play is set in the outdoors, use green posterboard and markers to outline trees and mountains on the side.

Each member of this charming cast is easily assembled over a wooden doll pin and chenille stem base. The puppets come to life when the magnets on their bases are set into motion by a magnetic wand inside the shoe box puppet stage. Create your own script, then watch the look of amazement on the faces of your audience when your puppets move on stage as if by magic to act out scene one.

The stage and these cast members are only a starting place for your child's creativity. Encourage kids to combine different colors of modeling material and chenille stems to create their very own characters. As children assemble their own puppets and props, they'll experiment with the principles of balance, weight and magnetic force. What a great learning opportunity!

Dragon Marionette

When you create this dragon marionette, both its finished size and animated presence will astound you. Styrofoam body pieces are connected with feather boas that are set into motion with the slightest of movements. The lifelike gentle giant will capture the heart and applause of any audience.

WHAT YOU WILL NEED

- ☆ two 4" (10cm) Styrofoam balls (for head)
- ☆ four 3¹⁵/₁₆" x 1¹⁵/₁₆" (100mm x 49mm) Styrofoam half spheres (for feet)
- ☆ 5⁷/₈" x 1¹³/₁₆" (149mm x 30mm) green Styrofoam disk (for front body)
- ☆ 8⁷/₈" x 1¹³/₁₆" (225mm x 30mm) green Styrofoam disk (for back body)
- ☆ 4" x 9" (10cm x 23cm) Styrofoam cone (for tail)
- ☆ four 4" (10cm) round wooden plaques
- ☆ 12" x 19" (30cm x 48cm) wide iridescent fabric
- ☆ craft foam scraps (for mouth and teeth)
- ☆ ¼" (6mm) diameter dowels, two 12" (30cm) lengths and one 30¼" (77cm) length

- ☆ two 24mm frog eyes (discard metal or plastic backings)
- ☆ 24" (61cm) feather boa (for front legs)
- ☆ 36" (91cm) feather boa (for back legs)
- ☆ 72" (183cm) multicolored feather boa (for back)
- ☆ twelve 2" (50mm) red pom-poms (for feet)
- ☆ four 1" (25mm) red pom-poms (for feet)
- ☆ two 1" (25mm) red pom-poms (for nose)
- ☆ two black mini pom-poms (for nostrils)
- ☆ straight pin
- ☆ wooden craft stick
- ☆ three bobby pins
- ☆ spool of mason line

- ☆ four 3/8"–16 x 1¹/₂" (1cm–16 x 4cm) hex head bolts
- ☆ spool of 24-gauge red wire
- ☆ serrated plastic knife
- ☆ tacky glue
- ☆ pencil
- ☆ scissors
- ☆ masking tape
- ☆ Styrofoam glue (I used Beacon Hold the Foam glue)
- ☆ hot glue gun
- ☆ patterns (page 87)

1 Use a serrated plastic knife to slice ¼" (6mm) off one end of each of the two 4" (10cm) Styrofoam balls. Tie one end of a 24" (61cm) piece of mason line to the middle of a craft stick. Insert one end of the stick into the cut side of one of the Styrofoam balls. Apply Styrofoam glue to the Styrofoam around the stick. Push the cut side of the second Styrofoam ball onto the other end of the craft stick. This forms the head.

2 Use a pencil point to poke a hole through the small disk 1½" (4cm) from the bottom. Then thread the 24" (61cm) length of boa through the hole to make the front legs. Repeat the process with the larger disk, poking a hole about 2" (5cm) from the bottom of the disk and threading the 36" (91cm) boa through the hole to make the back legs.

3 For the feet, use a pencil to poke holes through the centers of each of the four half spheres, rotating the pencil to enlarge the holes. Next thread one end of a 24" (61cm) length of mason line through each hole. Working with one of the front legs, thread the end of the boa through the hole in the half sphere foot, being careful not to remove the line. Repeat the process to attach feet to the three remaining boa legs.

4 Tie a hex-head bolt to the end of mason line below each foot. Push the bolt up into the base of the Styrofoam foot so that the head of the bolt is flush with the flat base of the half sphere. Use Styrofoam glue to attach a wooden plaque to the base of each foot.

6 Before assembling the puppet, lay the pieces out in order on your work surface. Start with the head, followed by the front body and legs, the back body and legs, and ending with the cone tail.

5 Use the pattern to cut the wings and combination eye/ear pieces out of iridescent fabric. Accordion fold the fabric wings and then position the center of the folded wings over the top of the smaller (front) body disk. Push a straight pin down through the folded fabric and into the Styrofoam to hold the wings in place. Fold the ear/eye piece according to the pattern and then make a small slit through both layers where marked. Thread the back of a frog eye through the slit in the folded fabric. Cover the plastic peg at the back of the eye with Styrofoam glue and then push it into the side of the head. The fabric ear should extend behind the head. Repeat the process to attach the second eye and ear.

7 Starting on the second half of the head, attach the multi-colored boa down the back of the dragon. Glue the boa to the Styrofoam with Styrofoam glue. Leave a few inches of unattached boa between each Styrofoam piece. Trim the end of the boa to stop at the end of the tail. Cut the remaining length in half and glue one half to each side of the boa that was placed along the large back body disk.

8 Cut three 24" (61cm) lengths of mason line and tie one end to each of the three bobby pins. Cover the bobby pin ends with glue, then insert one into the Styrofoam at the center top of the front body disk, into the back disk and into the tail.

9 To connect the dowels, lay the longer dowel vertically onto a flat surface. Place the shorter dowels 9" (23cm) from the top and bottom of the longer dowel. Tightly wrap a piece of wire around where the dowels intersect.

11 Cut the mouth and teeth from craft foam scraps; hot glue the teeth followed by the mouth to the end of the head. Hot glue two 1" (25mm) red pom-poms and two black mini pom-pom nostrils above the mouth. Hot glue three 2" (50mm) red pom-poms to the front of each foot and a single 1" (25mm) red pom-pom to the back of each foot.

10 Tape the center dowel to the underside of a table or chair so that when you attach the puppet strings to the dowel, the dragon's feet will touch the level surface of the floor. Loosely knot the strings for the head, front and back body, and tail to the center dowel. Attach the front feet to either end of the front shorter dowel and the back feet to either end of the back shorter dowel. Make adjustments, shortening or lengthening the strings as necessary, then tightly knot and trim the strings. Apply tacky glue to each of the knots to keep them from slipping.

THE WIZARD'S REQUEST

The boys followed Topaz and Garnet to the window ledge and watched in awe as the dragons grew to full size in the night air. Without hesitation each boy climbed on his dragon's back, taking flight in the moonlit darkness. After a few moments, the loud beating of dragon wings slowed to a single swoosh as they landed on an overgrown lawn in front of a crumbling stone castle. "Don't worry, you're safe here," said Garnet as she pulled open the arched door. A crackling fire welcomed them, warming their wind-chafed skin.

The boys were wondering what they'd gotten themselves into, when a friendly voice greeted them from the doorway. "Jasper and Elliot, welcome. I'm Lars. So glad you can help us."

"What can we do?" Jasper stammered, astounded at the sight of the imposing wizard.

"Follow me and I will show you." The boys followed Lars down the candlelit hallway as he explained that a crystal ball had been stolen from his tower, and without it, he could not monitor the balance between the magical and the real worlds. In his study he unfurled a map, and with his fingertip he traced a path from the castle to the land of the unicorns in the steep hilltops of the forest.

"But why us? How can we help?" Elliot asked again.

Lars studied the boys. "You've been chosen because Pearl, the youngest unicorn in the herd, will not trust an adult. Your minds are open to magic, and together you'll have the courage to handle whatever happens." Returning to the map, he continued to explain the journey. Once they had found Pearl, she would take them to the lake of illusions where they could retrieve a new globe. "We'll need to do something about your clothes," he said, as he passed them each a bundle with a cape, hat, lantern and wand.

"Wands?" exclaimed the boys. Lars replied, "Just in case."

bewitching COSTUMES

IN THIS CHAPTER YOU'LL FIND EVERYTHING YOU

NEED TO DISGUISE YOURSELF AS A WIZARD,

INCLUDING A REALISTIC WAND, CAPE, HAT

AND EVEN A LANTERN. IF YOU'D RATHER

BE TRANSFORMED INTO A MAGICAL

CREATURE, YOU CAN CHOOSE FROM A

VELVET BELLIED HORNED DRAGON WITH

SEQUINED WINGS OR A UNICORN COMPLETE

WITH FRINGED HOOVES, FLOWING TAIL AND A

WREATH OF FLOWERS. DRESSING UP HAS NEVER

BEEN SO EASY OR SO MUCH FUN.

Wizard Costume

Abracadabra, alakazoom! Cast spells all over your room! This complete wizard costume includes an elegant hat that is durable enough to withstand many adventures. The shimmering cape adds mystery to the ensemble, and the wand is a must-have for every aspiring wizard.

WHAT YOU WILL NEED

GENERAL
- ☆ scissors
- ☆ hot glue gun

Cape (page 43)
- ☆ 2½ yards (2.5m) of 45" (114cm) wide black/bronze lamé fabric
- ☆ liquid seam sealant (I used Dritz Fray Check)
- ☆ 2 yards (2m) twisted gold cord
- ☆ straight pins
- ☆ sewing machine and thread

Wizard Hat (page 44)
- ☆ witch hat
- ☆ permanent spray-on fabric glitter (I used Tulip Fabric Glitter Spray)

- ☆ 28" (71cm) of 1½" (4cm) black velvet ribbon
- ☆ 28" (71cm) of ⅞" (2cm) wide embroidered fabric trim
- ☆ moon charm
- ☆ 3½" (9cm) tassel
- ☆ needle and thread
- ☆ wire cutters
- ☆ newspaper

Wand (page 45)
- ☆ 3¾" (10cm) doll pin (standard size)
- ☆ chopstick
- ☆ medium wooden candle cup (⅝" [2cm] opening)
- ☆ spool of ⅛" (3mm) wide ribbon
- ☆ 2½" (6cm) piece of embroidered trim

- ☆ 10½" (27cm) suede lace
- ☆ double-stick tape
- ☆ craft glue or hot glue gun
- ☆ all-purpose industrial-strength adhesive (I used Aleene's Platinum Bond 7800 Adhesive)
- ☆ sandpaper
- ☆ masking tape
- ☆ tall drinking glass

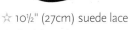

Cape

1 To make the cape, fold the 2½ yards (3m) of fabric in half so that the cut edges come together at the bottom of the cape. Working over a protected surface, apply liquid seam sealant along the bottom edges of the cape to prevent fraying. Pin the fabric layers together in a straight line 6" (15cm) from the fold. Machine stitch a straight seam across the line of pins, removing them as you work along the top of the cape. Next, make a second seam 2" (5cm) away from the first to create a channel for the gold cord.

2 Thread the twisted gold cord through the channel and knot the ends to prevent the cord from unraveling.

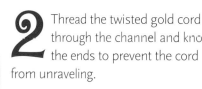

TIP
To make a smaller collar on the cape, in step 1 shorten the distance between the fold and the stitched channel.

Wizard Hat

TIP

The inexpensive base hat can be found in department stores with seasonal Halloween supplies in the fall or at theatrical supply stores year round.

STEP ONE

1 Loosely stuff the hat with newspaper so it stands upright for spraying. Working over a protected surface in case of overspray, spray several separate coats of fabric glitter over the hat. Allow the hat to dry completely before continuing.

STEP TWO

2 With wire cutters, snip the outer wire brim. With scissors, cut the brim off the hat. Be careful to leave the seam where the brim meets the hat intact so that the cut edge won't cause the remaining fabric to unravel.

STEP FOUR

3 Hot glue velvet ribbon around the base of the hat to conceal both the cut edge and the seam. Then hot glue decorative fabric trim around the center of the velvet ribbon.

4 Hand sew the tassel and charm to the top of the hat.

STEP THREE

44

Wand

STEP ONE

1 Apply three strips of double-stick tape around the doll pin. Starting at the top of the doll pin, tightly wrap the ribbon down the length to the base, covering the split in the pin.

2 Glue the base of the doll pin into a wooden candle cup.

STEP THREE

3 Glue a small piece of embroidered trim around the top of the doll pin. Apply additional glue to the cut trim end to prevent fraying. Wrap a piece of suede lace around the candle cup and then knot the ends.

STEP TWO

4 Rough up the flat end of the chopstick and the top of the doll pin with sandpaper. Apply a generous dot of industrial-strength adhesive to the top of the doll pin. Push the rough end of the chopstick down into the glue. It's a good idea to have another pair of hands to help with this last step. While someone holds the top of the chopstick and bottom of the handle, gently lay strips of masking tape from the chopstick down to the doll pin. Set the wand handle end down into a tall drinking glass and allow the glue to set 24 hours before removing the tape.

STEP FOUR

45

Wizard's Lantern

Illuminate your nighttime adventures safely with wizard style. This old-fashioned lantern is actually a soda bottle powered by a modern light stick.

WHAT YOU WILL NEED

- plastic 2-liter bottle
- 12" x 18" (30cm x 46cm) sheet black craft foam
- black electrical tape
- stickers
- 30" (76cm) of ¼" (6mm) wide twisted silver cord
- light stick, approximately 5¾" (15cm) long
- rubber band
- stapler
- scissors
- ruler
- pattern (page 88)

TIP
Use an adhesive remover, such as Goo Gone, to remove bottle labels.

1 Following the bottom seam, cut the bottom off the plastic 2-liter bottle and set it aside. Use a ruler to help position a rubber band 1½" (4cm) up from the cut base. Be sure the rubber band is straight, and use it as a guide to cut 1½" (4cm) off the base of the bottle. Discard this cut plastic piece and remove the rubber band.

2 Reconnect the bottom piece that was set aside in step 1 to the bottle, placing one strip of black electrical tape around the new seam. To form the lantern, lay five 7½" (19cm) tape strips from the top of the taped seam up to and under the bottle lip, lining one strip halfway between each bump at the bottom of the bottle. Lay five 2" (5cm) tape strips from the bottom of the taped seam to the base of the bottle, centering one strip on each bump. Wrap the bottle cap with black electrical tape.

3 Use the pattern to cut the lantern top out of black craft foam. Position the top of the bottle in the round center opening. Bring the foam sides together and overlap the edges. Staple them together once halfway down the shade and then again along the edge.

4 Randomly place stickers around the lantern. Tie the cord around the top of the bottle, then knot the ends together in an overhand knot to form a loop. Knot each individual cord end to prevent the ends from unraveling. Next, remove the bottle cap. Loop a rubber band through the hole in the light stick and insert it into the bottle, letting the top of the rubber band extend over the bottle's mouth. Replace the cap to trap the rubber band in place.

Dragon Costume

Astound your friends with this striking dragon costume. The hat is simple to make and comfortable to wear, with lightweight foam pieces assembled over a baseball hat. Once you've made the dragon, it'll be a breeze for you to make the unicorn, which shares the same basic construction.

WHAT YOU WILL NEED

GENERAL
☆ scissors
☆ hot glue gun
☆ sewing machine and thread
☆ patterns (page 88)

Body (page 49)
☆ sweatshirt (purchase sweatpants at the same time to complete the costume)
☆ 1 yard (1m) of 44"/45" (112cm/114cm) wide 100% polyester iridescent stretch velour
☆ 2 yards (2m) of 44"/45" (112cm/114cm) wide red sequined fabric
☆ 1 yard (1m) of 3" (8cm) wide gold upholstery fringe
☆ fiberfill
☆ straight pins
☆ needle and thread

Tail (page 51)
☆ three socks (women's size 9–11)
☆ fiberfill
☆ 9" x 12" (23cm x 30cm) sheet red craft foam
☆ 1 yard (1m) of 1" (3cm) wide black ribbed nonroll elastic
☆ 32" (81cm) of 3" (8cm) wide gold upholstery fringe

Head (page 52)
☆ two 1½" (4cm) Styrofoam balls
☆ two 2½" x 2" (6cm x 5cm) Styrofoam eggs
☆ black craft foam scraps
☆ three to four 12" x 18" (30cm x 46cm) sheets red craft foam
☆ red baseball cap
☆ metallic gold acrylic paint
☆ gold glitter
☆ 16" (41cm) of 3" (8cm) wide gold upholstery fringe
☆ stapler
☆ paintbrush
☆ paper plate (optional)

Body

1 Cut the velour 1½ times the width and length of the sweatshirt. Fold the fabric in half and lay it over one side of the sweatshirt. Cut through both layers of fabric to match the collar shape and taper the top half of the fabric sides from the waist to the arm/shoulder area. Trim the top folded edge to match the shoulder seams.

★ STEP ONE

2 Unfold the fabric and hot glue the top edge to the sweatshirt, starting with the left shoulder, working across the collar and ending with the right shoulder.

★ STEP TWO

★ STEP THREE

3 Make four horizontal folds down the length of the fabric over the front of the sweatshirt. The folds should increase in size as you work your way from top to bottom. When you're pleased with the length and position of the folds, pin them to the front of the sweatshirt.

4 Open the bottom of the sweatshirt and position it over the arm of the sewing machine, so that you sew through only the velour and the front of the sweatshirt. Make four separate straight seams along each line of pins, removing the pins as you work.

5 Stuff each of the folds with fiberfill. Bring the sides of the fabric down to cover the stuffing. Apply hot glue to the fabric edges and tuck them down against the sweatshirt.

6 For the wings, first determine the needed width of the red sequined fabric by measuring from one sweatshirt cuff to the other. Trim the fabric accordingly, and then fold the width in half. Cut four scallops through both layers of fabric along the open edge of the folded fabric. To shape the bottom of the wings, cut a 45° angle up toward the fold.

7 Unfold the wings and center the sweatshirt over them. Hand sew the center top of the wings to the back of the sweatshirt behind the collar. Next, sew the wings where they meet the outside edge of the shoulders (at the top of each sleeve). Then sew each wing tip to the corresponding cuff. This will anchor the top of the wings to the shirt but allow the bottom to swing freely.

8 Position one end of the fringe at the center back of the collar and then hot glue in place. Loop the fringe around the front of the collar, hot gluing it along the collar's edge as you wrap it back around to meet the glued end. Hot glue the remaining length down the center of the back.

Tail ★ STEP ONE

1 Stuff three socks with fiberfill. Join the socks into a long tail by inserting the toe of the second sock into the cuff of the first sock and the toe of the third sock into the cuff of the second sock. To secure the socks, lift up the cuffs and squeeze hot glue under them.

★ STEP TWO

2 Fold the elastic in half and insert the folded elastic into the cuff at the top of the tail. Machine stitch the top cuff closed, trapping the folded elastic in the seam.

3 Use the pattern to cut the tail tip out of red craft foam and hot glue it over the last sock. Hot glue upholstery fringe from the base of the tip to the top of the tail, separating some of the fringe to fall to the left and some to the right. Hot glue the separated strands to the socks. Wrap the elastic ends around your child's waist and tie them in a loose knot.

★ STEP THREE

51

Head

1 Working with one piece at a time, brush gold paint onto the two Styrofoam eggs (for eyes) and two Styrofoam balls (for nostrils). Cover most of the piece, but leave a small unpainted area for gluing onto the hat. While the paint is still wet, sprinkle gold glitter onto each piece and let dry. For easier cleanup, place the pieces over a paper plate while sprinkling the glitter.

★ STEP ONE

★ STEP TWO

2 Cut the eye pattern out of black craft foam scraps. Hold one of the eggs horizontally and apply hot glue to the back of a foam piece. Wrap the V around the center of the egg, positioning the open ends at the top and the point at the base. Repeat the process to attach the second V to the other eye.

3 Cut the head pattern out of red craft foam and then hot glue the nose end of the headpiece under the end of the hat's bill. Hot glue the round nostrils, unpainted side down, onto the bill so that they extend out from either edge of the nose.

★ STEP THREE

★ STEP FOUR

4 Bring the headpiece up and over the nostrils, hot gluing the underside where the cap meets the brim. Hot glue the end of the headpiece to the back of the hat above the adjustable strap.

52

5 Hot glue the eyes, v-shape out, onto either side of the hat. Fit the eyes partway under the head-piece, lining up the front of the eye with the seam between the bill and the hat.

STEP FIVE

STEP SIX

6 Use the ear pattern to cut out two red craft foam ears. Working with one ear at a time, fold the foam in half lengthwise and staple the folded layers together at the base of the ear. Hot glue the ear behind an eye, placing the glued end up against the underside of the head-piece. Repeat the process for the second ear.

STEP SEVEN

7 Use the horn pattern to cut two red craft foam horns. For each horn, squeeze hot glue down the length of the longest side of the horn and tightly roll the foam toward the point. Add more hot glue as you roll, squeezing the rolled foam for a few seconds while the glue sets. Continue rolling, gluing and holding until you reach the pointed end.

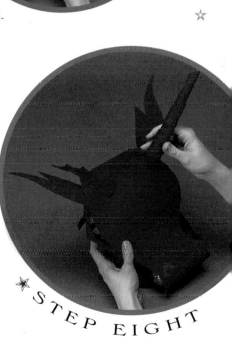

8 Pinch the top of the headpiece alongside an ear and snip an x-shaped slit into the foam. Insert the wide end of a horn into the slit. Repeat the process on the other side.

STEP EIGHT

STEP NINE

9 Hot glue the top edge of the fringe down the front of the finished dragon's head, positioning the folded end at the nose and the cut ends toward the back.

53

Unicorn Costume

Unicorns are the most elusive mythical creatures, and now you can transform yourself into one of these mysterious beauties. The pieces are easy to assemble with a stapler and glue gun. Purchase a leotard, tights and slippers to complete the costume.

WHAT YOU WILL NEED

GENERAL

- ☆ scissors
- ☆ stapler
- ☆ hot glue gun
- ☆ patterns (page 89)

Head (page 55)

- ☆ two 3" x 2½" (8cm x 6cm) Styrofoam eggs
- ☆ two 1½" (4cm) Styrofoam balls
- ☆ three 12" x 18" (30cm x 46cm) sheets white craft foam
- ☆ black and gray craft foam scraps
- ☆ white baseball hat
- ☆ white acrylic paint
- ☆ iridescent glitter
- ☆ 22" (56cm) of ⅜" (1cm) wide silver ribbon
- ☆ 18" (46cm) of 3" (8cm) wide blue upholstery fringe

- ☆ silk flowers (remove stems): two medium and one small white gardenias and two medium and one small blue daisies
- ☆ paintbrush
- ☆ paper plate (optional)

Hooves (page 56)

- ☆ 12" x 18" (30cm x 46cm) sheet white craft foam
- ☆ 34" (86cm) of ¼" (6mm) wide silver ribbon
- ☆ 16" (41cm) of 3" (8cm) wide blue upholstery fringe
- ☆ hole punch

Tail (page 56)

- ☆ 12" x 18" (30cm x 46cm) sheet white craft foam
- ☆ spool of 5¾" (15cm) wide tulle sold with bridal supplies (this will provide enough yardage to make the garland, as well)

- ☆ 1 yard (1m) of 1" (3cm) wide ribbed nonroll white elastic
- ☆ silk flowers (remove stems): seven white gardenias

Garland (page 57)

- ☆ six 45" (114cm) lengths of tulle left over from tail
- ☆ 4 yards (4m) of ½" (1cm) wide silver ribbon
- ☆ rubber band
- ☆ silk flowers (remove stems): seventeen white gardenias and blue daisies in varying sizes

Head

The unicorn's head is assembled like the dragon's (see pages 52–53), except for the following adjustments: The eyes and nostrils are painted white and sprinkled with iridescent glitter. Cut two unicorn eye patterns out of black foam and glue them over the center of each eye. Cut two gray foam eyelashes and glue them over each eye so they come out from under the white foam headpiece. Cut two ears out of white foam, fold them in half lengthwise and then staple the layers together at the base. Pinch the top of the foam headpiece and snip a 1" (3cm) straight slit onto either side of the head above the eyes. Insert the stapled end of one ear into each slit.

1 Cut a large horn out of white foam and then roll and glue it as for the dragon horns. Glue one end of the silver ribbon to the top of the horn and then spiral the length of ribbon down the unicorn horn, anchoring it to the foam every 1"–2" (3cm–5cm) with hot glue.

STEP ONE

2 Pinch the headpiece foam between the nostrils and snip an x-shaped slit. Insert the wide end of the horn into the slit.

STEP TWO

STEP THREE

3 Fold the blue fringe in half and hot glue the wrong sides together. Apply hot glue along the top edge of the joined fringe and glue it down the center of the headpiece, positioning the folded edge toward the front and the cut ends toward the back of the hat. Hot glue the white and blue flowers around both sides of the fringe. Place the larger flowers by the ears and the smaller flowers closer to the eyes.

Hooves

Tail

1 Cut the hoof pattern out of white craft foam. Punch two holes 3/8" (1cm) from each end. Hot glue an 8" (20cm) piece of the blue upholstery fringe to the top edge of the craft foam. Repeat for the second hoof.

1 Cut sixteen pieces of tulle off the spool at random lengths between 18"–26" (46cm–66cm). Fold each piece in half lengthwise and trim it at an angle so one end of each of the tailpieces is tapered. Cut the tail pattern out of white craft foam and then staple the center of the elastic to the bottom edge of the wide end of the foam tail.

2 Cut the silver ribbon in two and thread through the holes of each hoof. Tie the ends in a bow so they can easily be tied and untied.

56

2 Bunch the flat end of the tulle pieces together and lay them inside the tail base above the elastic. Roll the wide foam end over the tail-pieces, applying hot glue to each section of foam as you roll. Clamp the rolled foam in your hands while the glue sets. Squeeze additional hot glue into the top of the tail to help hold the tulle in place.

★ STEP TWO

Garland

3 Hot glue the white flowers in a circle around the top of the tail. Wrap the elastic around your child's waist, positioning the tail toward the back. Loosely knot the ends together.

★ STEP THREE

1 Cut three 45" (114cm) lengths of ½" (1cm) wide silver ribbon. Lay out three piles, each consisting of two 45" (114cm) lengths of tulle and one length of ribbon. Bind the piles together at one end with a rubber band, but keep them separated for braiding. Loosely braid the piles together. When finished, bring the bottom of the braid up to the top to form a loop. Remove the rubber band and tie the ends together with a short length of ribbon.

★ STEP ONE

2 Apply hot glue to the back of the flowers and several small leaves. Tuck them into the folds of the braided tulle, gluing the smaller flowers around the top, which will wrap around the neck, and the larger flowers around the center, which fall in the front.

★ STEP TWO

THE LAND OF THE UNICORNS

Just over there," Garnet motioned to Topaz. Topaz nodded his head as they angled their wings for a landing in the narrow clearing at the edge of the woods. The boys climbed down, rubbing their eyes as they adjusted to the darkness. Topaz leaned toward their lanterns and blew a spark to ignite them. "You're not going to leave us, are you?" Elliot implored.

Garnet lowered her eyes and pulled out a shining scarlet orb pendant and placed it over Elliot's head. Topaz did the same for Jasper, placing a brilliant blue orb around his neck. Topaz explained, "If you need us, hold the pendants and we'll come." Quietly the boys watched as the dragons flew off into the starry night.

Feeling determined, Jasper said, "Elliot, let's look at the map and get started." Much later, tired and scratched by the underbrush, the boys were ready to stop and catch their breath by a cave. They flattened the map against the rock. By lantern light, they determined that they'd almost made it to the land of the unicorns, when they heard laughter. "Did you hear that?" Elliot whispered. "I think it's an owl," Jasper reasoned. But when they heard it again there was no question; it was laughter. They ducked into the cave, and Jasper quickly covered the lanterns with his cape. The boys watched in silence as tiny goblins passed by the mouth of the cave. Deciding the coast was clear, the boys raced out of the cave and up the path, anxious to find Pearl. When they crested the hill, they could see down into the valley.

"There she is," Elliot whispered as he pointed to the smallest of the majestic creatures grazing away from the rest of the herd. As they approached Pearl, Elliot picked a daisy stem from the field and lifted it to her. Gingerly she took the flower and looked questioningly at the boys.

"Pearl, will you take us to the lake of illusions?" Jasper asked. "Lars has sent us to bring back a crystal." Pearl lowered her front legs to let the boys climb on, then racing at a gallop she rose into the sky.

Spellbinding
PARTY

THIS CHAPTER IS FILLED WITH IDEAS TO MAKE YOUR WIZARD PARTY MAGICALLY FUN. WRITE INVITATIONS ON FOLDED DRAGONS WITH MOVING WINGS. WHEN YOUR GUESTS ARRIVE, HAVE THEM DECORATE THEIR OWN WIZARD HATS. RAISE BEJEWELED GOBLETS FOR A TOAST AND THEN EAT CAKE OFF FIRE-BREATHING PLATES. ENTERTAIN YOUR GUESTS WITH A SPARKLING BOARD GAME CRAFT AND THEN TAKE TURNS PLAYING THE FINISHED GAMES TO COLLECT CHOCOLATE COINS.

Dragon Invitations

These dragon invitations will surprise your friends. When unfolded, they'll triple in size and raise their wings to reveal your written invitation. Even if you don't have party plans, send a friendly note on this dragon to brighten someone's day.

WHAT YOU WILL NEED

- ☆ 8¹/₂" x 11" (22cm x 28cm) colored cardstock
- ☆ 8¹/₂" x 11" (22cm x 28cm) colored vellum
- ☆ 5³/₄" (15cm) x 4³/₈" (11cm) envelope, one for each card
- ☆ small oval wiggly eyes, two for each card
- ☆ mini brad, one for each card

- ☆ fine-tipped black marker
- ☆ gold metallic marker
- ☆ silver metallic marker
- ☆ tacky glue
- ☆ pencil
- ☆ scissors
- ☆ standard hole punch

- ☆ ¹/₈" (3mm) hole punch
- ☆ patterns (page 90)

NOTE: Additional postage may be required. Please have your finished card weighed at the post office.

1 Trace the body and ear patterns onto cardstock and the wings onto vellum. Cut two ears and two wings. Use a standard hole punch to make a nostril at the end of the nose. Use a fine-tipped black marker to outline the inside edge of the dragon, then draw a row of pointed teeth under the nostril, ending in an upturned smile. Flip the card over and duplicate all the black lines. On both sides of the card, use a gold metallic marker to outline the pointed tip of the tail, and then use a silver metallic marker to outline the punched nostril and fill in the teeth.

STEP ONE

2 Using the fold lines on the pattern for reference, fold the head over toward the tail and then crease the fold line with your fingertips. Repeat the process, folding the tail down toward the head.

STEP THREE

STEP TWO

3 Glue an ear to the front and back of the head. Then glue an eye to the front and back of the head.

4 Stack the wings together and position them along the dragon's back. Use a ⅛" (3mm) hole punch to punch through the vellum and cardstock layers. Insert a mini brad through the punched hole to join the pieces together, then separate the metal ends and push them flat against the back of the invitation. Once connected, the wings can be posed in different ways. Fold them down over the writing to fit the card in the envelope.

STEP FOUR

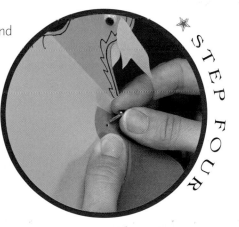

Wizard
Party Hats

These instant wizard hats—only minutes to fold—
will put any partygoer in a festive mood. They're
also a quick solution to any costume party
dilemma. If you don't have an art store nearby
that sells colored paper by the yard, substitute
white paper or sheets of newspaper and
draw the stars with black markers.

WHAT YOU WILL NEED

☆ 19½ x 28" (50cm x 71cm) black paper
   (or use newspaper and color it with
   black permanent marker)
☆ gold metallic marker
☆ stapler

STEP ONE

1 Randomly draw stars and moons over one side of the paper, using a gold metallic marker.

STEP TWO

2 Place the paper horizontally in front of you, drawn side facing down. Fold the right side toward the left at a diagonal. The top of the flap should measure approximately 11" (28cm).

STEP THREE

3 Fold the left side over toward the right, forming a diagonal that meets the first fold at the top to make a pointed tip.

4 Bring the folded edge on the right side toward the middle of the hat, keeping the point at the top, and then flatten this last overlap.

STEP FIVE

5 Insert the stapler into the hat and staple the top folded layers together with a single staple. Gently roll up the uneven ends to form the hat brim. Adjust the brim to fit the wizard; roll the paper higher to accommodate bigger heads.

STEP FOUR

Jeweled Goblets

Gilded and sparkling with jewels, these goblets are sure to make you feel like royalty. The combination of acrylic plastic glasses, strong glue and waterproof paint markers makes this drinkware durable enough to last through many feasts and festivals.

WHAT YOU WILL NEED

☆ plastic wineglasses

☆ plastic rhinestones in assorted sizes and shapes: circles, hearts, stars

☆ silver and gold waterproof metallic paint markers

☆ all-purpose industrial-strength adhesive (I used Aleene's Platinum Bond 7800 Adhesive)

☆ masking tape

☆ adhesive remover, for mistakes (I used Goo Gone)

NOTE: The decorated goblets are waterproof and can withstand the dishwasher, but hand washing will extend their longevity.

TIP

If you make a mistake, wipe it away with an adhesive remover, wash the cup and start over.

STEP ONE

1 Use paint markers to draw the following motifs around the goblet: a circle of sun rays, a single crescent moon, a straight wand stem, a straight line with a loop at the top and a bumpy end at the bottom to make a key, and an outline of an eye shape. Color the length of the wineglass stem solid gold.

2 To complete and accent the drawn motifs, use industrial-strength adhesive to attach the following rhinestones around the goblet: a large circle in the center of the sun, small stars next to the moon, a star at the top of the wand, a large and small heart under the top loop of the key, and a large circle in the center of the eye. Immediately apply a strip of masking tape over each glued rhinestone to hold it in place while the glue dries. (Without the tape, the rhinestones will slip down the side of the goblet.) Remove the tape after the glue has dried.

STEP TWO

These goblets are the perfect companion to the Dragon Plates on page 68.

Dragon Plates

Set a truly magical party table with these dragon plates. Each dragon breathes curling ribbon fire and flies with a pair of gold paper napkin wings. One small plate makes the body, and a second plate is cut to make the head and tail. The assembled dragon sits on a large gold charger plate.

WHAT YOU WILL NEED

☆ colored paper plates, two small colored and one large gold per dragon
☆ gold paper napkins, two per dragon
☆ curling ribbon
☆ brads, one per dragon
☆ pencil

☆ paper clip
☆ scissors
☆ paper punch
☆ tape
☆ tacky glue
☆ patterns (page 90)

2 Glue the head and tail face-down onto the back of the second small plate, positioning them so the cut spines on the center plate make a connection between the head and the tail.

1 Trace the head and tail patterns over the back of a small plate, being sure to line up the patterns along the plate rim. Use the paper punch to punch the marked eye and nostril in the dragon's head. Cut a row of spikes along one-third of the second plate rim.

3 Insert a brad into the punched eyehole, separating the metal ends behind the head. Cut two small lengths of ribbon and then carefully curl them against the open scissors blade. Tape the ribbon ends to the back of the mouth so that the extending curled ribbon gives the illusion of fire.

4 Hold a napkin diagonally in front of you and fold each side down at an angle under the napkin. Repeat with the second napkin and then use a paper clip to hold the pointed ends together, making a set of wings. Position the paper clip between the finished dragon plate and the larger gold plate so that the napkin wings extend up from the dragon's back.

Adventure Game

Have your guests create and play with their very own board game. Patterns and stickers make assembling the game a breeze. Precut the paths and scroll shapes (see step 1, page 71) for your guests before the party. Have dice, inexpensive rings and foil-wrapped chocolate coins ready to accompany each finished playing board. Your guests will be eager to take this favor home to play additional rounds with their families.

WHAT YOU WILL NEED

☆ 8½" x 11" (22cm x 28cm) colored cardstock

☆ 8½" x 11" (22cm x 28cm) adhesive felt or foam for backing (I used Sparkle Foam)

☆ stickers: unicorn, celestial, castle and dragon motifs

☆ dice

☆ rings, to use as play pieces (I used silver and gold rings sold as wedding favors)

☆ foil-wrapped chocolate coins

☆ gold metallic marker

☆ fine-tipped black marker

☆ glue stick

☆ scissors

☆ patterns (page 91)

1 Use the pattern to cut the path and scroll shape out of cardstock. Mark the place lines on the path with a gold metallic marker. Use the fine-tipped marker to outline the scroll and to list the following key instructions down one side of the scroll: power of the crown +4, shooting star +3, cast spell +2, sunshine +1, nighttime -2, collect coin.

STEP TWO

2 Apply glue to the backs of the scroll and the path and then position both pieces onto a plain sheet of cardstock.

STEP THREE

3 Press stickers onto both the scroll and path. Glue the underside of the game onto the backing. If you use adhesive foam, peel off the paper to reveal the adhesive. Carefully attach the backing to the underside of the board, working from top to bottom to prevent air bubbles.

Game Instructions

Roll the dice and move your ring playing piece that number of spaces along the path. If you land on a space with a sticker, check the key to find out what to do next. You might get to pick up a chocolate coin or have to move a specified number of spaces forward or back. It's hard to say whether the winner is the first to reach the end of the path or the one who picks up the most chocolate coins. If you come up short on chocolate, don't worry. The more you play, the more coins you'll collect.

SAFE PASSAGE HOME

They awoke to see the dawn breaking over a mist-covered lake.
They landed by the shore, Elliot gently stroking Pearl's neck as
she caught her breath. "Where do we find a crystal?" Jasper asked.

Pearl motioned her head to the water and spoke for the first time.
"Look carefully." Staring through the rising fog, the boys saw bubbles
floating over the water surface. "Each of those is a crystal."

"But how do we get one?" Elliot asked. "You'll have to use magic. Good luck,
friends," she said as she galloped in flight back toward her home.

They watched until she was just a faint sliver against the pale sky and then turned their attention
back to the water. Elliot wrapped his hand around the wand in his pocket and wondered aloud if
they could use them to lift a crystal. "It's worth a try," replied Jasper. "Let's pick that one by the
edge." Lifting their wands, they aimed them at the crystal, which responded by splashing out of
the water. Eyes big, Jasper quickly directed Elliot, "I'll hold it up. You run over there to catch it."

Elliot darted down to the shore and stretched his arms up to the crystal, which fell into his
hands. Captivated by the radiating warmth, he peered into the swirling glass. Jasper came to
his side. "We need to get it to Lars. Let's call for Topaz and Garnet." Elliot nodded in agreement
and gently placed the crystal in his lap as he joined Jasper grasping his pendant in his hand.

Late that morning Jasper awoke in their room to find a spell book by the bed.
When he opened it, a feather pen rose and began writing the potion for the
unicorn apparition. Jasper's excitement woke Elliot, who opened his eyes to find
Garnet returned to her original size beside his pillow, her gleaming eyes blinking.

Magical GIFTS

EVERYONE COULD USE A LITTLE MAGIC. SHARE THE

GIFTS IN THIS CHAPTER WITH FRIENDS AND FAMILY.

IF YOU'RE IN A HURRY, THE DRAGON AND

UNICORN T-SHIRTS ARE QUICK AND EASY

TO MAKE. THERE'S ALSO A DECEIVINGLY

SIMPLE-TO-MAKE ORB PENDANT. IF YOU'RE

MAKING A GIFT FOR SOMEONE WHO LOVES

TO WRITE OR DRAW, CHOOSE THE SPELL BOOK

WITH A COORDINATING FEATHER PEN AND LET

THE RECEIVER FINISH THE CREATIVE PROCESS.

Spell Book

Gilded embossed letters are mounted onto decorative papers, transforming an ordinary notebook into a volume worthy of a place in any wizard's library. You can fill the pages with sketches, stories or journal entries. And don't forget the elegant coordinating bookmark (see page 77) to save your place.

WHAT YOU WILL NEED

GENERAL
- ☆ letter stamps
- ☆ metallic gold acrylic paint
- ☆ liquid polymer clay, optional (I used Liquid Sculpey)
- ☆ acrylic or plastic roller
- ☆ paintbrush
- ☆ paper towels
- ☆ oven
- ☆ craft glue

Spell Book *(page 77)*
- ☆ ½ block polymer clay
- ☆ 4³/₄" x 5½" (12cm x 14cm) spiral sketchbook (or use a ruled notebook)
- ☆ 5½" x 4½" (14cm x 11cm) adhesive-backed sparkle paper (I used Making Memories sparkle paper)
- ☆ 3⅛" x 2³/₄" (8cm x 7cm) suede-textured cardstock
- ☆ dragon stamp

Bookmark *(page 77)*
- ☆ ⅛ block polymer clay
- ☆ 1³/₄" x 8½" (2cm x 22cm) adhesive-backed sparkle paper
- ☆ 1³/₄" x 8½" (2cm x 22cm) scrapbook paper
- ☆ 1¼" x 7³/₄" (3cm x 20cm) suede-textured cardstock
- ☆ 14½" (37cm) of ⁷/₈" (2cm) wide black ribbon

TIP

☆ *Supervise your children when using an oven.*

1 Work the clay in your hands to smooth the ridges and make it more pliable. Roll the clay into a 2" x 2½" (5cm x 6cm) wide shape. Rough edges will help the finished piece look aged. Press a dragon stamp into the top of the clay, then spell out a book title with the letter stamps under the stamped dragon. Bake the clay according to the package directions. For extra durability, brush a thin layer of liquid polymer clay onto the clay before baking.

2 After the clay has cooled, brush metallic gold acrylic paint into the imprinted image, letters and rough edges. Rub excess paint off with a dry paper towel. Don't be concerned if the paint smears; it'll add sheen to the black clay.

3 Remove the paper from the sparkle paper to expose the adhesive. Center the sparkle paper on the front of the notebook. Use craft glue to adhere the textured cardstock on top of the sparkle paper. Finally, glue the back of the polymer clay piece onto the textured paper. Allow the glue to dry completely before opening the cover.

For the bookmark, make a square shape with rounded corners from the clay. Gently pinch the top and bottom sides together and then the left and right sides for a less uniform shape. Press the letter stamp into the center of the clay and bake as directed. Next, repeat step 2 above. To assemble, back the sparkle paper with scrapbook paper. Cut a v-shaped notch in both ribbon ends and extend the ends evenly above and below the sparkle paper. Glue the center section of ribbon that overlaps the film. Glue the clay piece to the top of the textured cardstock, then glue the cardstock over the center of the ribbon.

Orb Pendant

This pendant is the master of disguise. It's simply a marble wrapped in wire and decorated with a small silver charm. A standard bag of marbles offers a great selection of potential pendants, but if you're looking for something truly unique, visit a toy shop that has a display of collectible marbles. The choices for charms are just as great. Once you start making these pendants, you'll never run out of inspiration or grateful recipients.

WHAT YOU WILL NEED

- ☆ marble
- ☆ 15" (38cm) 24-gauge wire for a shooter-size marble or 10" (25cm) for a standard marble (I used Fun Wire)
- ☆ metal charm
- ☆ 24" (61cm) black cord
- ☆ scissors

1 Fold the wire at 5" (13cm) from the end and then place the marble in the fold. Wrap the wire around the marble. Tightly twist the wire ends together at what will be the top of the pendant.

2 Bring both of the wire ends down and twist them again at the base of the marble.

3 Bring the ends back to the top and twist them one last time. You should have six bands around the marble. Bend the shorter wire end into a loop and then wrap the very end around the base of the loop. Thread the longer wire end under all the bands, then bring it up to the base of the loop and spiral it down around the combined base of twisted wires and wire end to conceal them. Continue wrapping, working your way down to the marble, making progressively larger circles. Stop when you're left with 3/4"(2cm) of wire.

4 Thread the charm onto the remaining wire and then continue wrapping the wire around the top of the marble. Tuck the wire end into the wrapped wire. (If you're concerned that the wire will pull out, dot the end with jewelry glue before inserting it into the wrapped wire.) Thread a piece of cord through the wire loop and knot the ends.

79

Dragon Crystal
Ball Holder

You will treasure this thing of beauty, whether or not you can see the future in the swirls of glass. The polymer clay dragon has shimmering scales of miniature marbles, wire claws and metal wings. Permanently wrapped around the glass candleholder, he'll always protect the crystal ball.

WHAT YOU WILL NEED

- ☆ one block of purple polymer clay
- ☆ 24-gauge wire (I used Fun Wire)
- ☆ tiny marbles
- ☆ rhinestones, two small black and two medium purple
- ☆ large glass marble
- ☆ glass candleholder

- ☆ lightweight aluminum sheet (I used ArtEmboss)
- ☆ plastic knife
- ☆ scissors
- ☆ pencil
- ☆ oven
- ☆ patterns (page 92)

T I P

☆ *Supervise your children when using an oven.*

1 Use the dividing marks in the clay to separate two quarter blocks for the body, one quarter for the head, and one quarter divided into three pieces to make two front feet and one back foot. Work the sections in your hands to soften and blend the clay before shaping the pieces.

2 Mold the head and feet onto the body, carefully smoothing all the connections with your fingertips. Insert the knife blade into the end of the head to separate the upper and lower mouth.

3 Cut nine 1" (3cm) long sections of wire for the claws. Curl one half of each wire into a rounded claw shape. Press the straight end of a shaped wire into the clay foot, placing three claws on each foot. To make the spikes, bend the wire into waves, and to gauge the length, hold the bent wire over the dragon and make adjustments before cutting it off the spool. Insert the wire end into the nose and then push the bottom of the shaped wire down the length of the back and tail. Where necessary, smooth the clay over the wire connections so that the wire spikes appear to emerge unconnected from the clay.

4 Press tiny marbles into both sides of the dragon. Press two small rhinestones into either side of the nose for nostrils. Press a pencil eraser into either side of the head to make two eye sockets. Set a medium-size purple rhinestone eye into each socket. Use your fingertips to gently push the clay over the rhinestones' edges to secure them.

5 Partially wrap the dragon around a glass candleholder, leaving the head and tail end posed away from the glass. Lift the inside front leg up against the side of the glass.

6 Use the patterns to cut the wings, ears and fire out of lightweight aluminum. Insert the wings into either side of the wire spikes on the back. Fold the flat end of the ears and insert them behind the eyes. Bend the fire up and down and then push the flat end into the back of the mouth. Bake according to the instructions on the polymer clay package. Be careful when moving the finished dragon; pick up the glass candleholder and the dragon together. When cool, set the large marble on the candleholder.

STEP SIX

Experiment with different clay, marble, wire and metal colors to make your favorite dragon. Topaz is wrapped around an inverted votive holder that has an indentation in the base.

If the crystal ball doesn't shed light on a situation, switch the marble to candles. With adult supervision these dragons can create a magical candlelit mood with flickering light reflecting off their metal wings.

Feather Pen

The ultimate wizard writing accessory, the feather pen is the perfect companion to the spell book. This modern version is much easier to use than real quill pens that were dipped in ink.

WHAT YOU WILL NEED

- ballpoint pen
- metallic embroidery floss
- 10"–14" (25cm–36cm) white quill
- 1/2" (1cm) wide double-stick craft tape (or regular double-stick tape)
- scissors
- clothespin
- craft glue

STEP ONE

1 Remove the pen's cap and apply a strip of double-stick tape to each side of the pen. Press the sides of the tape around the pen so that the surface is covered. Peel off the colored film to expose the adhesive surface. Place the end of the embroidery floss on the tape about 1/2" (1cm) up from the bottom tape edge. Bring the floss down to the tape edge to start wrapping. Work your way up the pen, wrapping over the floss end to trap it in place. Once you reach the top, cut the floss and glue it over the last wrap.

2 Cut the quill end off the feather. Apply craft glue to the quill of the feather, about 3" (8cm) up from the bottom. Press the feather to the pen, positioning it under the top 3" (8cm) of the pen. Clamp the feather to the pen with a clothespin while the glue dries.

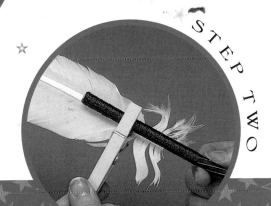

STEP TWO

Magical T-Shirts

This project requires absolutely no sewing but gives the appearance that it's professionally made. When choosing fabrics for the dragon or unicorn, check the wide selection of cotton fabrics intended for quilters. The dimensional paint edging is both decorative and functional, preventing the cut fabric edge from fraying.

WHAT YOU WILL NEED

- ☆ cotton T-shirt (prewash)
- ☆ fusible web (I used HeatnBond Ultrahold)
- ☆ fabric scraps (prewash)
- ☆ silver and gold dimensional metallic fabric paint (I used Tulip Dimensional Metallics)
- ☆ small ribbon rose (for unicorn only)
- ☆ stud with prongs

- ☆ rhinestone setter or flat-head screwdriver
- ☆ pencil
- ☆ scissors
- ☆ iron
- ☆ fabric glue (for unicorn only)
- ☆ patterns (page 93)

NOTE: Prewash both the T-shirt and fabric scraps to remove the sizing that is placed in the fabric during manufacturing.

T I P

☆ *Supervise your children when using an iron.*

1 Follow package instructions to iron the fusible web to the back of the fabric scraps. (For the unicorn, use only one fabric piece.) Trace the dragon and wing patterns or the unicorn pattern onto the paper backing and then cut out the pieces.

2 Peel off the backing and then lay the dragon or unicorn, adhesive side down, on the center front of the T-shirt. Iron the creature to fuse it to the T-shirt. For the dragon, position and iron one wing at a time so they extend out from each side of the dragon.

3 Before painting on the T-shirt, test the dimensional paint flow and practice making lines on a fabric scrap. Once you have a feel for the paint, slowly outline the dragon with silver paint, extending a claw out from the center of each toe. Next outline the wings with gold dimensional paint and squeeze a dot onto the end of the nose for a nostril. Leave the finished shirt lying flat so that the paint doesn't smear, and allow it to dry completely overnight. (For the unicorn, outline the body, mane, tail and mouth with silver dimensional paint, and the neck, horn, hooves and nostrils with gold. When dry, glue a ribbon rose above the neck using fabric glue.)

4 For the eye, push the stud into the head through the front of the T-shirt. Working on the inside of the T-shirt, use a rhinestone setter or flat-head screwdriver to flatten one prong at a time down into the fabric to secure the eye in place.

patterns: **enchanting toys**

Stuffed Dragon, *page 22*
☆ Enlarge these patterns by 152%.

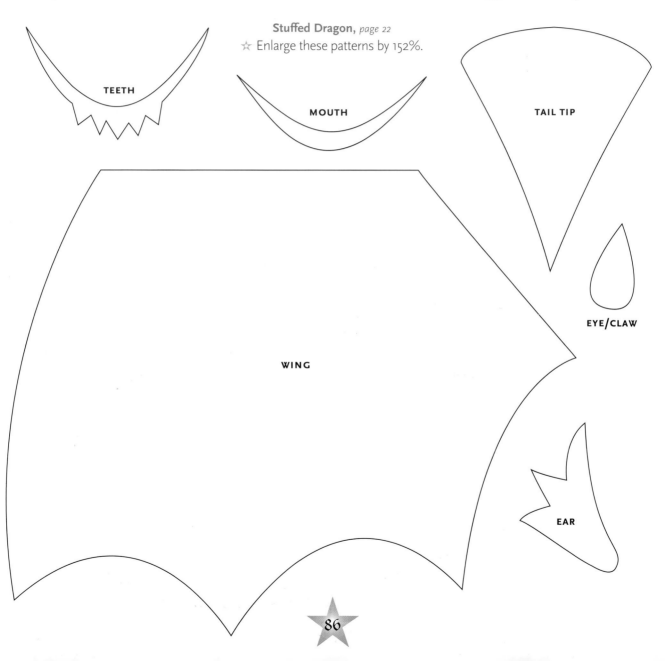

TEETH

MOUTH

TAIL TIP

EYE/CLAW

WING

EAR

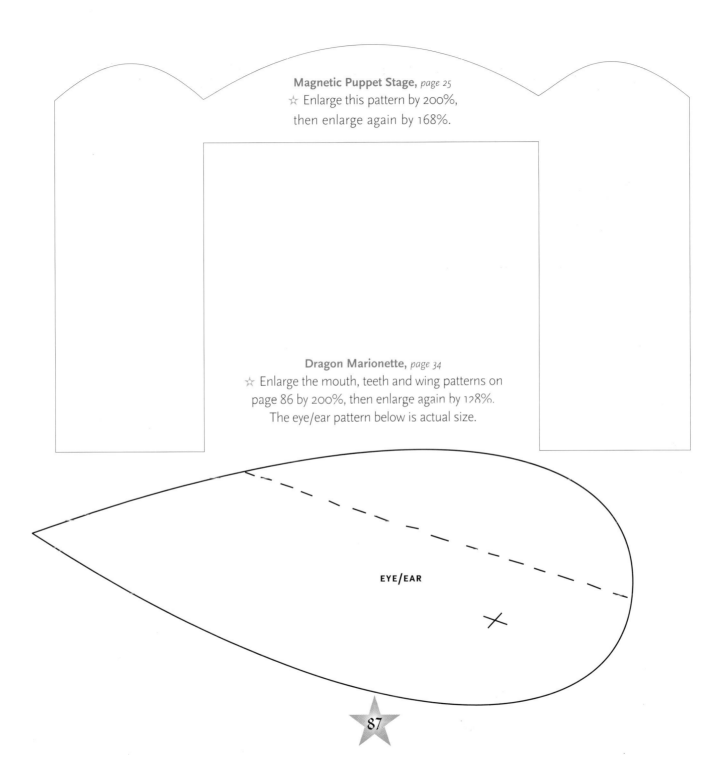

Magnetic Puppet Stage, *page 25*
☆ Enlarge this pattern by 200%,
then enlarge again by 168%.

Dragon Marionette, *page 34*
☆ Enlarge the mouth, teeth and wing patterns on
page 86 by 200%, then enlarge again by 128%.
The eye/ear pattern below is actual size.

EYE/EAR

patterns: **bewitching costumes**

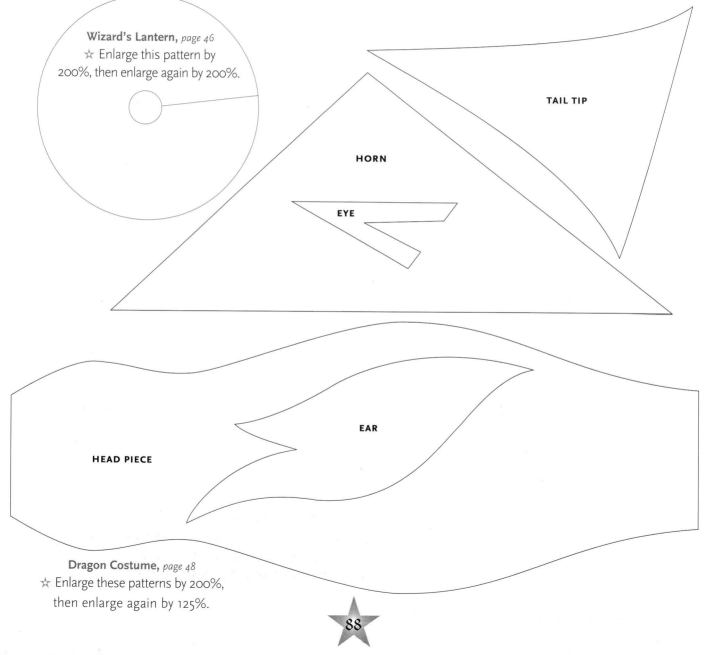

Wizard's Lantern, *page 46*
☆ Enlarge this pattern by
200%, then enlarge again by 200%.

TAIL TIP

HORN

EYE

EAR

HEAD PIECE

Dragon Costume, *page 48*
☆ Enlarge these patterns by 200%,
then enlarge again by 125%.

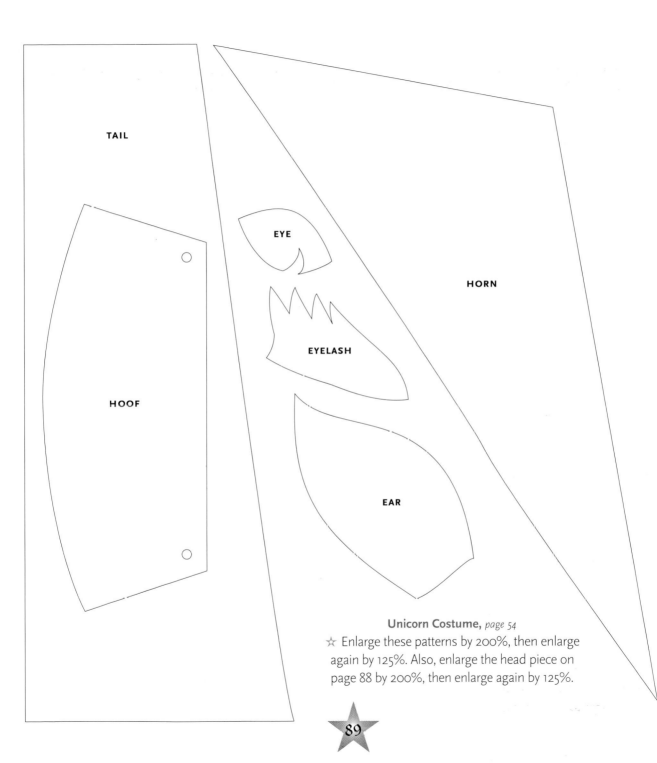

TAIL

HOOF

EYE

EYELASH

HORN

EAR

Unicorn Costume, *page 54*

☆ Enlarge these patterns by 200%, then enlarge again by 125%. Also, enlarge the head piece on page 88 by 200%, then enlarge again by 125%.

patterns: **spellbinding party**

Dragon Invitations, *page 62*
☆ Enlarge these patterns by 200%.

EAR

WING

BODY

TAIL

HEAD

BODY

Dragon Plates, *page 68*
☆ Enlarge these patterns by 200%.

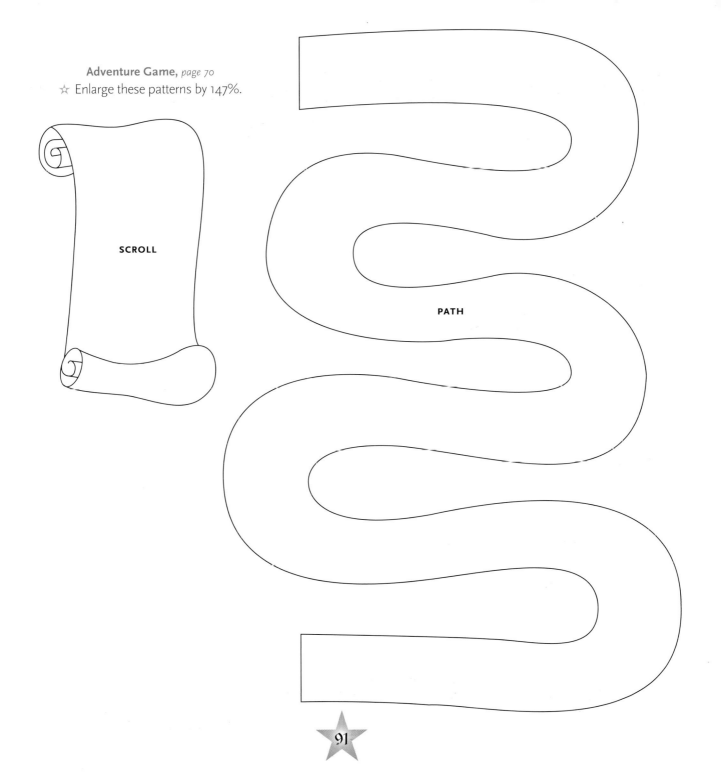

Adventure Game, *page 70*

☆ Enlarge these patterns by 147%.

SCROLL

PATH

patterns: magical gifts

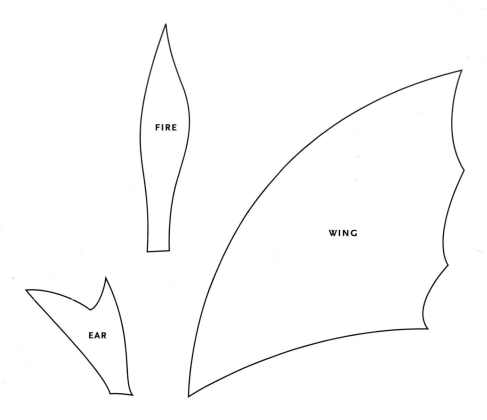

FIRE

WING

EAR

Dragon Crystal Ball Holder, *page 80*

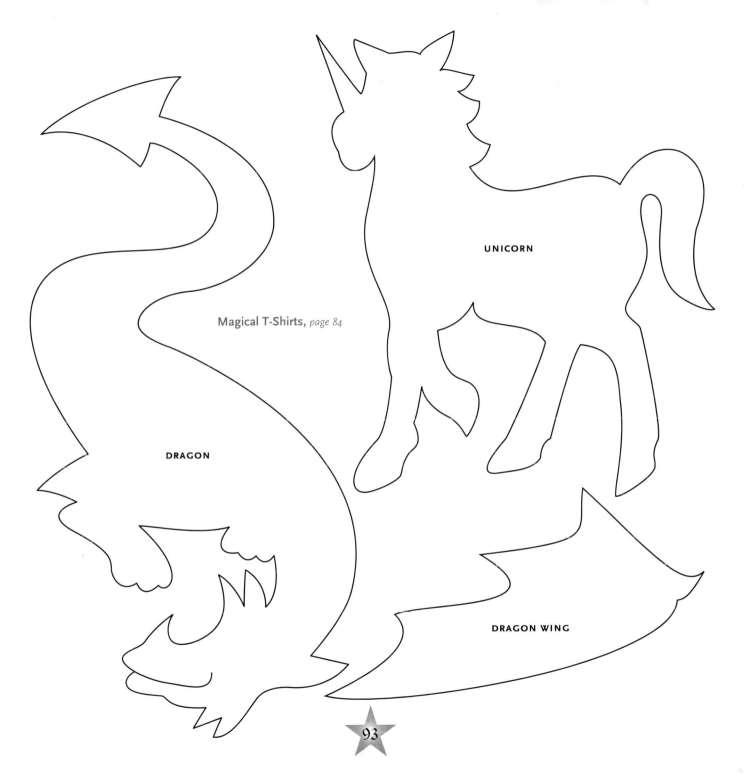

UNICORN

Magical T-Shirts, *page 84*

DRAGON

DRAGON WING

93

★ resources

AMACO
American Art Clay Company, Inc.
4717 West 16th Street
Indianapolis, IN 46222
(800) 374-1600
www.amaco.com
☆ ArtEmboss

Beacon Adhesives Company, Inc.
125 South MacQuesten Pkwy.
Mount Vernon, NY 10550
(800) 865-7238
www.beaconcreates.com
☆ Hold the Foam, Kids Choice Glue

Binney & Smith, Inc.
1100 Church Lane
P.O. Box 431
Easton, PA 18044-0431
(800) 272-9652
www.crayola.com
☆ Crayola Model Magic

Delta Technical Coatings
2550 Pellissier Place
Whittier, CA 90601
(800) 423-4135
www.deltacrafts.com
☆ Delta Metallic Gold Acrylic Paint

Duncan Enterprises
5673 East Shields Avenue
Fresno, CA 93727
(800) 438-6226
www.duncancrafts.com
☆ Aleene's Platinum Bond 7800
Adhesive, Aleene's Tacky Glue,
Tulip Dimensional Metallics Paint, Tulip
Fabric Glitter Spray

Halcraft, USA
30 West 24th Street
New York, NY 10010
(212) 376-1580
www.halcraft.com
☆ tiny glass marbles

Making Memories
1168 West 500 North
Centerville, UT 84014
(801) 294-0430
www.makingmemories.com
☆ sparkle paper (self-adhesive)

Polyform Products Company
1901 Estes Avenue
Elk Grove Village, IL 60007
(847) 427-0020
www.sculpey.com
☆ Sculpey Polymer Clay

Prym-Dritz Corporation
P.O. Box 5028
Spartanburg, SC 29304-5028
(800) 255-7796
www.dritz.com
☆ Dritz Fray Check

Therm O Web
770 Glenn Avenue
Wheeling, IL 60090
(847) 520-5200
www.thermoweb.com
☆ HeatnBond Ultrahold fusible web

Toner
699 Silver Street
Agawam, MA 01001
(413) 789-1300
www.tonerplastics.com
☆ Fun Wire

index

Get creative with these kids craft books from North Light Books!

Painting on Rocks for Kids

Hey kids! You can create amazing creatures, incredible toys and wild gifts for your friends and family. All it takes is some paint, a few rocks and your imagination! Easy-to-follow pictures and instructions show you how to turn stones into something cool—racecars, bugs, lizards, teddy bears and more. ISBN 1-58180-255-2, paperback, 64 pages, #32085-K

Puppet Mania! Springboard your imagination on a fantastic puppet-making adventure! Renowned puppeteer John Kennedy will show you how to make 13 cool puppets, including Bottle Bug, Boxing Kangaroo, Dancin' Chick and Nutty Bear with easy, step-by-step instructions. You'll also learn how to bring your creations to life through lip-synching, body movement, eye contact, and your imagination! ISBN 1-58180-372-9, paperback, 80 pages, #32386-K

Stamp Your Stuff! You'll be the envy of all your friends once you learn how to Stamp Your Stuff. This cool craft technique makes it easy to express your true personal style. Whether you want to jazz up your room or create a hip little fashion accessory, this book shows you exactly how to get there. You'll learn how to create one-of-a-kind bracelets, bulletin boards, lamps, greeting cards and more! ISBN 1-58180-386-9, paperback, 64 pages, #32432-K

Clay Characters for Kids

Mold polymer clay into a fantasy world right out of your imagination! Maureen Carlson shows you how to sculpt 10 easy shapes that can be used to create dozens of different creatures and characters, including dragons, goblins, fairies, ghosts, pigs, dogs, horses, bunnies and more. ISBN 1-58180-286-2, paperback, 80 pages, #32161-K

These and other fine North Light titles are available from your local art & craft retailer, bookstore, online supplier or by calling 1-800-448-0915.